ESCAFELD HANGINGS

Escafeld Hangings

Geraldine Monk

WEST HOUSE BOOKS 2005

Published by
West House Books, 40 Crescent Road
Nether Edge, Sheffield s7 1HN, UK
www.westhousebooks.co.uk

Distributed in USA by
SPD, 1341 Seventh Street
Berkeley CA 94710 - 1409
www.spdbooks.org

Typeset in Bembo Book at Five Seasons Press, Herefordshire
and printed on Five Seasons one hundred per cent
recycled book paper by Biddles Ltd, King's Lynn

ISBN 1 904052 17 7

*West House Books acknowledges
financial assistance from*

For my lovely and lovely great-nieces
Olivia & Saskia

Contents

8

PART ONE

The City of Eternal Construction

'The town is being torn down and rebuilt at an immense speed.'

George Orwell on Sheffield 1935

Darren de Lovetot

'So what',
I ask the lad in the baseball cap and bling,
born-n-bred in the catchment area,
'is or was Escafeld?'

'You're asking the wrong question',
he mumbles aslant,
'It's whether Thundercliffe woz under u cliffe or struck more
than twice wiz a weird sort o gad-light and the ultimate big noise—
are we talking Thor or . . . or Cindercliffe', he went on, 'Where did that
come from? One place: so many names.'

'But Escafeld?' I insist, '*Ash field* not Sheaf has been suggested by an
Anglo-Saxon scholar called Bill.'

'Wicked!' he said or maybe it was 'Wicker'.

We both stare
into the
middle distance
of
yonder.

'There are so many angles' he mused and turned.

Did he mean angles or Angles? Before I could ask Darren slouched off
into one of the seven hills suddenly hooded and outlawed.

I turn but catch the rush of dreaded words:
'*check id out.*'

Idid.

Incunabula aka Swaddling Clothes

And Escafeld begat Sheffield with
sideshows & outreaches

HALLAM   ATTERCLIFFE
                        TICK HILL
HANGING WATER
            SPOUT SPINNEY
                        WINCOBANK
    BROCCO BANK
                              BRINCLIFFE EDGE
NETHER   EDGE   NETHER   GREEN
        BELL HAG   HAG HILL   HALLOWMOOR
CROOKES
            MOORFOOT
                    PITSMOOR
SKYE EDGE   GOOLE GREEN
                                    SHIREGREEN
                    BURNGREAVE
MEERSBROOK
            STUMPERLOWE   RINGINGLOW
                                    FIRTH PARK
BEAUCHIEF   OSGATHORPE
        LOXLEY   TOTLEY
                                    PHILADELPHIA
                    RIVELIN
ATLAS   UNDER TOFTS
        GRIMESTHORPE   BRIGHTSIDE   GREENLAND
SNIG HILL   STAGGER LEES
            SHARROW
                    SPITAL HILL   CORKER BOTTOMS
WISEWOOD   WINDLE   NORTON LEES
                ARBOURTHORNE
        PARSON CROSS   CROSS POOL
    BIRDWELL   SWALLOWNEST   OWLERTON
HEELEY   WHIRLOW   KILLAMARSH
                HUNTERS BAR
    OUGHTIBRIDGE   HAIL MARY HILL
                WICKER
                LADYBRIDGE
                CASTLEBECK
                WYBOURN
                MANOR

Downing the Days

At a rough guess the foundations
are under the fish and meat markets
and extend beneath the law courts.
Within these precincts the Scottish Queen schemed
and plotted and ordered the latest
French fashions
suffering
agonies of ages—
deferred
hope—
endless embroideries

her red-raven locks turned grey

before the key forty life
began begging
with an eloquence to
warm the feet of our
mongers and butchers
wallowing in the traces of
her damp
lodgings—
cleaving away another
day.

'I do suffer her to walk in the ayr and
my large dining chamber.
I or my wife always keep her company' The Scottish Queen's Gaoler

English weather tones—
wreckers of damasks.
Huntswoman cuts a
wren-soft
marrow-dash across
cheap chinaware—

a rustic scene to sup from—

cocker spaniel runs aflame
amongst heraldic icons
worrying
all the bunions down centuries
of women's feet
plodding their varicose and
purpose purse
to market
to market
to buy a fat
market-forced
scrag end o' beast on
the altar of
special offers.

Stall holders huddle
and pile up pies to
tempt
Satan and
Northerners alike in
their loving of
warm blooded living.

Let us pause before
the bread baps, spare ribs,
crab sticks and pigs trotters
consider hard this castle beneath our time
and plastic shopping bags:

Sheffield Castle and Manor

The Castle of Sheffield
fairly built stony and spacious
rose rude from gently rising ground
at the confluence of rivers
Sheaf (Sheath) and Don (Dun)
abounding with broad accent of salmons,
trouts, chevins, eels and
other fin things
bandaging the ramparts
from Lady's Gate to Waingate.

Entranced from the south fold
a gloomy so-it-says gateway
massive or mastiff with tooth and nail
portcullis
hung ready to chop off intruders.

Inside: stables, divers houses,
divers lodging, a granary barn,
inward-looking courtyards
and doubtless a cheerless dungeon.

Doubtless.

Outside: the hop-yard, cock-pit,
deer park and deep venison
chorus of orchards sporting the
largest trees in the country:
one oak stood on the conduit plain
forty-five feet from trunk-to-twig
capable of sheltering 200 horsemen.
Squirrels (red) can branch it 7 miles
without touching earth.
A magnificent avenue of walnuts
and oaks run riot to Shea bridge.

Uphill a manor
was built
in the modern
manner.

In these two dwellings
Mary,
Queen of the Scots,
lived and loathed
a lock-in for fourteen years
incredulous of dark stories
exposed to all the winds
and injuries of unfulfilled seconds.

'I call it her abode and no captivitie nor scarce a restraint
when in effect the greatest part of this realme was her prison
at large' The Scottish Queen's Gaoler

The hunting lodge alone remains intact
amongst the Manor's ruins.

The Castle fell to Cromwell's men:
the fossilised foundations
come up for air with each attempt
at urban redevelopment.

Tunnel Spottings

The City is mythically riddled.
Subterranean tunnels.
Human burrows from the Cathedral
to the Castle from the Hall in the Ponds
shooting up Manor Lodge through
Skye Edge from Priory Road
to Beauchief where wild wedding parties
are frowned upon
with further rumours
they tickle the outreaches of the city.

Cut from solid rock beneath
The Star of evening
news travelled quick to the
Tramway Club.

In 1936 in the midst of
a depression Frank Brindley wrote:
'My friend worked the cellar
during the now dead *Tissue*—
a race paper.'

'He saw', says Frank, quoting his mate,
'the man in ancient dress with
curious blood like history'

"'It' came through an unused cellar
and walked clean through stone.'

'He thought,' said Frank, quoting his mate,
'it was his mate but it carried a curious
bucket as if with water.'

Other tunnels have been sensed and spotted
and should not be undermined.

Under the Crown Court built on the castle
site they run like imaginary lines of freedom
teasing the feet of the convicted.

In Court No. 1 the ushers watch
the lamp suspended by chains:
'While the others remain motionless
this lamp swings gently
back
and
forwards
twisting one way then the
other'.

Habeas Corpus!

And still they run:
along the route where
t'Hole in th' Road underpass
descended into
a hell of a post-war bad idea
bristling zero degree hairs on warm
summery nights when a company
of friends couldn't soothe
the afterlingerings of hurt.
Afterlingerings that stank.

A warren of mugrape and lesser air.
They found the tunnels shocking . . .

. . . and closed them quick.

Frank Brindley did not rest.
He called in skilled masons:

'We found the missing tunnel
which no one in our times had seen
and what I call the 'ghost tunnel'
has a well worn floor from long
usage and bone
dry without
trace of rubbish . . .
its first direction was east towards
the Rising Sun then slight south
then east again.

One rock was writ with 'I.W. 1830''

Frank concluded:
'It is beyond all reasonable doubt
that this is the tunnel in the old papers.'
Running from the Earl of Shrewsbury's
'tash in the Lady Chapel through
the corners of Norfolk Row to
her Lady's twitching skirts
in a corner of the old cold Castle.

It is an absolute fact that last
century before last someone's
grandfather told him it was an absolute
fact the Scottish Queen had entered
Sheffield via a tunnel. He found the tunnel
which stunningly undered Heeley Bottom.
He'd been there. Done that. Got the absolute.

These snaky ructions
black as
Bertie Bassett's
innards
are still disputed
amongst masons
who freaked
at the depth of design
and
sudden gust of tunnels
clean cut
through uncuttable matter
lower
than
any
sewer.

The Lady Chapel—Sheffield Cathedral

Here lies our man Shrewsbury
                              worried to death
by Elizabeth
                    Mary
                            and his wee-wife Bess
staring up in perpetuity
            at the sheela-na-gig
spewing forth her seeds
            she is unashamedly not
(as the vergers insist)
                    a medieval acrobat
doing a twist
        w-hey she wears no knickers
                    and it's a strange trick
        for a circus artist
to spew seeds from a place
                surrounded by green men's
astonished heads
                            teetering between
                crossed swords
playing over and again the
    'beheading game'.

The Beheading Game

In Grenoside they dance
the glancing blow
of Winter's throes
with mock decapitation.

The captain wears a hat of fur
—preferable a hat of hare—
the sun will come to kill
this most magical
of bunnies.

The captain is a doomed man
his head crowned by the hexagram
of long swords and sordid sounds
to drown his round of
please and pleas.

They weave the geometric spell
but never break the lock and cell
to let the backdoor spy survive
'cause bound
and bound he is to die.

Before the kill
the ritual
they draw their swords
across the neck with
hex and grind and clash
of feel that honed-to-real
Sheffield steel.

The hat of hare
like Mary's wig
with dreadful lock
is lifted big and clean
or thrice a hack away
away the delicate neck—
haul away—

from anchor.

Connective Tissue

After three weeks
Jack the landlord of
the Manor Castle pub
next to the Sheffield Manor
quit.
The whole family
quit.
After three weeks.

Jack saw something and
besides he said it was as
though there was
somebody always
beside it was
always
as though there was
somebody else
beside
always as
though you were
always
beside
never on your
own
as though there
were somebody
always somebody
else
besides
you
were
never on
your own.

We went together.

To be alone.

PART TWO

Mary Queen of Scots

'I have seen some Rings made for Sweet-hearts with a Heart enamelld held between two right hands. The Heart was 2 Diamonds which joined made the Heart. Queen Elizabeth kept one mœitie and sent the other as a Token of her constant Friendship to Mary Queen of Scotts: but she cutt of her Head for all that.'

John Aubrey

Unsent Letters

Scandal Letter

Madam, Goode Queen Bess,

I shall declare to you now sincerely and without passion whatever—a man slept with you on countless occasions and you do not marry they say for never would you surrender a freedom to take new lovers in your hot-bed. You behave shamelessly with several at your chamber door in your chemise and as we know night gowns naught. My gaoler's wife advises me, laughing strongly, to place my son in the queue to make love to you. Further, after you slapped Killigrew for not bringing back your scared-stiff lover you insulted him about certain gold buttons for his doublet. It is the talk of the court. The sniggers behind the arras set whole narratives a-tremble with shaking shoulders.

I hear you have a high opinion of your beauty as if you are a goddess. And I don't mean domestic. Unreasonable flatteries pleasure you as none dare look at you in the face as it shone like the sun. And your ladies daren't but look at each other in the eye for fear of bursting out laughing at the flatter-lies they tell you.

They mock you as you break their fingers and strike their hands with knives at the dinner table. They mimic and mock you in comedy. And rage against your tyranny and green-spiked matchmaking.

You have irrational confidence. Predictions in a picture book shine upon our legs. How is the ulcer?

If I could speak to you at this moment, this moment, this moment, this moment, this moment, I could prove to you the truth.

I keep silent for your friendship is always on a promise.

From my bed, forcing my arm despite the sickness to satisfy and obey you.

A bad-hair day if ever,

Your sweet coz the Skottyshe Queene

Airport Security

Madam on High,

It is November. It is 1571. It is beyond a joke. My people are not permitted to go beyond the castle gate. Rumours a-go-go: tightened security at airports. It matters not to me: the one over the hill is so flightless. Another is planned. Dickie Bird Airport. It is a local joke of sorts. Bats, vampires, umpires, crickets. Something like that. I'm a stranger in a strange land. I don't get it.

I get cherry seas with dash't turquoise. Salt splayed on swell. Rogue waves thick as a cliff never melted butter in my mouth. But this lack of movement I cannot endure.

Beef. Confined to my chamber. To skirl the flying hawks from turret-top a seldom granted whim they wish again to wall up my windows and make a false door through which to enter my sleeping body.

Why while my body sleeps? Do they seek a sleep-stalked-loose-talking confession? T'place a mirror to my mouth and pray it doesn't mist? Feel my bosom as it heaves to stock-still? Robin-bloody-Hood! He came from here—did you know that? Robin the Tyke in Tights. You couldn't make it up. You couldn't make *me* up. Mary Queen of Scots banged up in the slammer in Sheffield.

Lizzy mi Luv call off yr creepsy guards. Abused sleep I need not on top of meat so sad and thin it ruined Easter Day and every thin day since. I don't complain. Mardy Mary me? Mi foot! My cross I bear in regal silence. I rail only at the half-seen sun.

I beseech you grant all heavenly benedictions and me all patience and consolation.

Sithee—as they say in these parts—Sithee?

Mary-Mary Quietly-Queeny

Menagerie

Madam, Goode Siſter,

The days I await your reply congeal to a slough of all ebb all ebb. I feel so
flaming *low-f-low*. Upon despond my life blood flues down one leg and
up the other. In the small hours I fret with threads in the bed linen—snags
irritate me—loose ends are an abomination—shoddy cotton is the dodo-
decline of civilization. In the small hours I count three types of blood
vessels—arteries—weather vanes—caterpillars. My blood courses withershins
and creepy-so. I do not dare lay sound upon my pillow for the loud of false
ſtop-ſtarts of heart alarms mi lugs.

If this is to be human I'd rather be fungi loving it up in the damp dark—
touchyfeely spores in the undergrowth. I'm hungry. I slice my life into three.
In reverse order I see England. Scotland. France. I see no further tranche.

The moon is a globe like earth but deader but not deader than my eyes.
Morf! D'ſt know? Duſt. The skeleton is what is left after the insides have
been taken out and the outsides taken off. It is something to hitch meat onto.
I wish mine was unhitched. Meet me now. Please. Or. Unmeat me now. Duſt
me.

I amuse myself after a fashion. Prod trivia. Toy with food. Slink a glance
and spy my eye in wine glass dregs on the cusp of night. Raspberry pools.
Fools of Scottish raspberries. Red as. Bring out yer dead. Eye makes a wild
fancy-frouer. Whiſtling pipe to decoy the winged ones. Little girl glows in
m'oldering body.

The equator is a menagerie lion running around Earth through Africa beyond
soft lovely France—rhubarb is celery gone bloodshot the night after the night
before—a vacuum is a large empty space where the Pope lives. No? You are
not amused? My reduĉtio ad absurdum raises not a titter? Not One Arf? Not
Three? Arf. aRfraF. afaR*ff*.

This is what I have become.
To: keep: milk: from: turning: sour: keep: it: in: the: cow:

:::::::::::::::::::::::::::::::::::::::

Your colon-d and semi-confeĉted coz
Maw–Maw the Scot

Casket Letter

Mighty, Hi Coz,

My five unequal branches are unequalled but substrata-spirits knarl as I write sore amazed. These branches that received a swell ring from you so true did usher an assurance of safe keeping. Third finger left hand—ha! So many obscure words and dark sentences come from England. Would I baffle with a long casket letter? Would I? Even though the casket be of silver and the notes on parchment rare. Nay. No one can compel me to accuse myself. I show little sign of grief yet it nips me near. *Nips me near. Rare near . . .*

Do not as the serpent that stoppeth his hearing for I am no enchanter but your sister and natural cousin. I am not of the nature of the Basilisk and less of the chameleon to turn you to my likeness. I continue to stitch pictures till very-pain makes me give over. This is my life. They have not yet built Ikea over the road. Rumour has it they never will. So I wave bye-bye to my dreaming flat-pack Trojan Horse. And stitch on. In anagram.

Veritas Armata

Lay Your Apples Like Eggs

Yer Maj,

If I could seethe till tender as Neats Tongues turned to Hash my days would not stick in my throat. I'm brittle as a Prince Bisket imbued with Butter as thin as you can then battered into bakers coffins. It streatches my choler. I begin to think in food and dwell on past feasts. It turns my pallor to a marble of Pomme-Cittron As They Do Beyond The Seas.

Send me confected Snow beaten with a birchen rod topped with a Sprig set in the midst a Sallet of Rosebuds and Gillyflowers in a pipkin with Roasted Carp Caper-rowlers of Radish Cods Cowslip Tart Larks Sparrows and Arrowroot to soothe the Pottage of Teals and Woodquests with Hypocrast to move my bowels.

Right now I need a Cawdle For A Sick Body Egg-Egg-Limon-Egg and the weak Honey drink made with taking warm fountain water scummed with a silver spoon and a feather.

Lard me with Lemon and cook me alive as they did-do with a goose— sponging his head and heart as his inner parts roasted till he run mad up and down and stumbled with his cooking juice roiling to the verge of language. My gnawing hunger for anywhere but here takes me in strange ways—

Caraway Caraway,

Affectionate Jumballs,
Mary Maw

Mutability Hall

Sweet Lilibet,

Good morrow. Mi marrow. Mi back. Mi hand back and forth exclaims in blue. Tut bone. With squiggly red thread veins. And liver spots. Lineage herbs go a-missing. Have you brought forth yet my pet? May your bundles of joy be without beginning.

Hereon these words come as blogs and baby-babble. I'm that way out. Way out my century. Way beyond my age. You get my driftseed?

Mutability is all the rage: The wane of the moon is rehired by local cowboys. Ah! Men on horseback. And side-saddled women. The best builders are from Rotherham. All De Lovetot's lads I suppose. They built this cold castle for my back. But a des-res is promised. A dry Manor on a high hill. But here in Mutability Hall old and cold go hand in threadbare glove. Ah Sheffield. As the locals say, 'It'll be alright when they finish it'. Sheffield's got restless soil.

Oh womany-womany. Year-stores of womb-quimbles. Restless soil.
My son I never see. A fat load of good to a fat womb that was.

Cold to the breeches,
Rubbing hands for the warmth of a letter,

Mary-in-Waiting

Buffer Zone

Sweet Coz, Higher than Higher,

You're a living thing!

But still no word from you? All I hear is the Williams sisters are ruining women's tennis as one old buffer on the airwaves said verily they are becoming a 'freak show'. I kid you not kin these weirdish words mean nothing to me but do not surprise the length of my weary imprisonment and wrongs I have received from those whom I have conferred so many benefits. An annoying annoyance beyond a hey-nonny-no. And ones who whitter in the wings when women sing with strong legs and serve to volley whomever it may concern into the middle of next week with good graciousness and knock-out beauty should know better. Get real my girl. You must have heard I'm lame and less a threat. My timbers shiver. My hair's gone to grizzle.

God keep you from misfortunes. The realities of my calamities and injuries done to me in various ways grant me patience and a deuce of match points flame up Lucifer's nose. I mean no harm. My shed is my shed. My lips are sealed.

Your obliged and affectionate good sister and coz at your pleasure and infinite leisure at your service or vice as it be versa. Is this your prison or mine? Time after time?

Marie Rrrrrrrrrrrrrrrrrrrrrrrrrrrr

Tremors

My Dear Highness, Hen,

Yesterday, in this year of 1574, an earthquake shook Sheffield out its boots in sundry places. It sunk chiefly my chamber. My gaoler says I was 'aferde'. Poppycock! I was gladdened to the quick. For the earth to suck me in would be a glee. And a nithering chill of excitement to fill a day is anything but amiss. But why do I fear February so? The month of deadening? La lune. Ma moon. Forms lakes.

My legs tremor without quake. I need no external uprush. The pain in my side is a metronome. Tickerty-blockerty. A gloom of waxwings settled on my pinhead. They are rare visitors to Sheffield. Crested angels in droves. They will land on Crescent Road one day. When they build the road.

The cawing of mead moils and bedlam spawned. Manchurian Sikka Deer— they roam. And winged insects out of season. My sixth sense has serifs. I binge-drink outta my leather bootees every Friday neet. Jeez my coz. This is one helluva asbo you've slapped on me. It's the existence I live by. Boredom I die by.
Groove-grieving.
Please release me from this Northern Ing of sway and twang.

Your toots lovin sis.
Mar–Mar

Feathers of America

To the High and Mighty Etcetera,

I salute your intelligence even though that very word doubles its bluff with false wars and sexes up a damp squib to apocalyptic tyrannical paranoia—I get carried away before I am carried away but before I am carried I must acquaint you with my state as briefly as can be: my batteries are going flat. The feathers from my Byrds of America are losing colour with my absence. This is no light matter.

Apropos of nothing. Is this the 'beautiful game' my voices speak? Two queens squaring up noses cross nor/sou divide beneath t'transit of Venus? The sun sunders under-clout never putting fangs or milk pegs forth in this godforsook sunlessland to cut a dash and toast the heart full score. This sentence is too long. Too. If this is a game—is it in two halves? And who's the referee? You may have heard I'm going deaf from lack of laughter.

My days weigh with interminable seconds. I pick up knowledge beyond my years. An inferno breaks my sleep. A centre of steel will tentacle around my spectral feet. Helium lights before my eyes. A falsetto skirl of flares will vanish in decades. Whowoossh.

With nothing in my present to engage I read the past and future terribly. I cry nightly for the Buffer Girls. Diamonds in brown paper. Ada. Oh. Lived-in lovely Ada.

I have taken up arms against my me. By unexpected means I try to die driven by the devil knows what horns. Almighty Disposer please deliver me recorded and urgent. I have lost the battle the war the want and loyal friends fell before my eyes could stop the unfold. I have no hope but for goodness with grace I cannot imagine the back of beyond nor see the broad streets of my afterlife. I miss my feathers

       dearly,
Your affectionate sister,

Millithrum Queet Spick

Looking Fingers

Yo! High Sissypuss,

Cat got yer tongue? Let's get one thing straight: we have all 'looked through our fingers' on expedient death. Oh yes. Our street fighting age and back-daggerings makes a mug of *all* our presumed innocence. So rickety glass-houses and big stones to you. Greeting-ghosts woman! What do you take me for? A croon of macaroons gone off? Some half-baked-biscuit basket case? Give me a break.

And hey—come up and see me sometime. Peel me a bloody grape. Let's go West and sassy. Seriously. Incarceration stinks high as Tutbury middims and Sis that stink still lingers in my silks and stomachers and I tell you now that's an awful lot of *s's* so let's go for plain anglais by saying it's **s-h-i-t-e**. *Pardon my French*.

I throw an attitude of distraction. My soul is wreathed with innermost tubes—red salmon pink—my tired insides stretch with scratch of yearn. This is *nodda* good day to be *me*. Write me I implore. Your silence is crashing. You *must* know:
a woman in prison lives in her postbag.

Humble humble all the rest da-di-dah,
Marie R

Crashworthy Ermines

Madam, Goode Sis,

The ſtone walls ſteer a diſtraction then ſtare back. Can a mind pass my life by and leave a body wholesome? The meat is bad with rancid fat as I grow gauche and ſtringy and a monody of crashworthy ermines sways from the rafters and furthermore sways to a chanson some ſtocking-woman sang as a chit.

This is what a mind does mid mindless onrush.

At firſt glance the words gave up a syſtem shock on reading 'several hands' as 'severed heads'—it speaks a maybe sleight of eye or worried mind or both conspiring on the side of darker plurals. There is nothing worthwhile I can do: Ask misery to cease? Being punished in a world like this my portion's in eternal bliss.

God speed the menopause.

Toots now,
Minging May. Query. Scots

Ava Va Va

Lizzykin, Poppet, My Pet,

I've seen swine flying in the peelings of onions. Who is playing Judas on this Hogmanay? What am I, alas, what use my life? I am nothing but a body without a heart, a vain shadow, an object of misfortune, that wants nothing but to die. Ava va va. When I went to the castle door and tirled at the pin they kept the key of the castle and would not let me in. Ava va va. Who learns my carol, and carries it away?

I took my foot in my hand and hopped o'er to Ingerland and you don't give a bawbee about me. Ava va va. I wish I was a Ladybird: Lady-lady Landers. I'd take up my cloak above my head and fly away to Flanders. Ava va va. O'er firth and fell, pool and well, moor and mead, living and dead, corn and leas, river and seas, east and west, fly to love, fly to best. Ava va va. Who learns my carol, and carries it away?

And tell me this Sis am I the one in the count-out rhyme? She lookit east, she lookit west, she lookit where to light on best, she lights upon a bank of sand to see the cocks of Cumberland. White pudding, black trout. I'm out! Am I so out that I'm in or so in that I'm out? Ava va va. Who learns my carol, and carries it away?

Wash well the fresh fish and skim well the bree there's many a foul-footed thing, many a foul-footed thing, in the salt sea. Soon your fury will be satisfied. Muckle ganging muckle ganging. Ava va va. Who learns my carol, and carries it away?

The new year brings a rain of peas and beans and the wind skirling like a kenna-whit, waking sleeping folk and the dead,

I wish again I was,

Hush-a-ba, birdie, croon, croon,

Ava va va,

Tu As Martyre

Cabin Fever

Madam, Dearest,

In the wee hours my heart crawls to the edge of the sheets and dangles by a thread.

One thought alone that brings me harm and good mingles bitter sweet within my heart without end, oppresses me until peace and rest flee from me, keeps me between doubt and hope. So, dear sister, if this paper expresses the insistent wish I have to see you, it is because I live in torment and sadness, if quickly it does not bring the desired effect.

Meanwhile I attempt escape. There is nothing so exquisite that I desire. To be free. Sadsweet mournful tune I cast a piercing glance upon my insufferable loss. I move from place to place but in vain. I see me in the water as in a tomb.

We suffer cabin fever in this castle. Scoff away. The bound body is a bind if the mind knows the body is bound. Get my drift. Arrest is arrest whether it be in pen or palace. Banish me to a bedsit but unlock the door.

I have seen a ship go out of control on the high seas, just before entering harbour and clear weather turn foul. Thus I remain in fear and anxiety, sometimes Fortune cruelly breaks our sails and double rigging.

Orisons to horizons to be reached,

Marie R

Our Violet-Pale Faces

Queenie E,

On a rare cool. Calm spikes impending. When I lie quietly sleeping upon my couch I hear you speak to me. Within my heart and eye lies a picture that shines forth our violet-pale faces—the colour of lovers.

My portrait shows the world my hurt—rising till it bursts a third eye in my furrowed brow. Always dreading the secret riffs of those brilliants abroad beneath my wall slats probing my spaces in this dark this silly mid-off land. We are caught between the plague on both our castle keeps and khazis. Yes my pet even my most privy moments are spooked with ears and eyes. And so are yours.

I will not accuse any person since I know your heart touches my blood. Enemies will slake their black disconsolate thirst on my white plasma. As I suffer this country I suffer you to remove my corpse to holy ground with a sacred geography and liberty to dwell in peace in my afterlife and France.

In respect to our consanguinity,

Queenie M

Points of Colour

Chère El on High,

Water. Sea anemones. Creature-me emotional in deep worry-dives. Sea
scythes. Scissors to my land-tongue. I am sub rosa. My world is in a state of
hush. And yet my body skrikes. Blue blud is no fortress against purple urine.
Porphyria. Canterbury bells. Palma violets. At what point exactly does blue
bleed into purple? Mauve to lilac? Rose to red? What is the point? All day
and every I paint with needle—the diversity of colours makes time seed
less tediously. I continue till the pain bleeds green to aquamarine to cobalt
twiligh . . . t . . . sky.

Oh my pure English rose.

My crew is diminished. I know not what line to sail nor how to lift my
anchor. Me—so at home on the sea. Now so landlocked. A gormless lubber
without a gull . . .

Codes lumpen inert. Stump me up Scottish tweed twinset wi freshwater
pearls. Family pact my pet. I need a perk. So what if the younger gives with
two hands what the elder gives with one finger. Since when has gifting been
a digit count?

I think more and more of before. Before this. How I have had to sleep upon
the ground and drink sour milk and eat oatmeal without bread and have
been three nights like owls, with no female companionship. Like owls is like
free.

My heart hopes to die cleanly but my ever diminishing octaves condense
into a low-throated curse. And here comes the inconsolable scratch of quill
at the final loop of my signature.

Tu Te Marieras

She Kept Birds

Emberiza citrinella

may-the-devil-take-you
writing master
scribbling lark
pretty-pretty-creature
yellow amber
yorling
yoit
yowlie
yite
gouldi
gladdie
bessie buntie
yedda yeldern
guler

Aegithalos caudatus

long-pod
millithrum
french pie
mumruffin
bellringer
prinpriddle
chittering in a
poke pudding
puddney poke
bum barrel
bush oven
can bottle
hedge jug

Pyrrhula pyrrhula

hoop hope
olf
nope
mwope
mawp
pope
bull sprink
bully
thick bill
blood olp
billy black
black nob
bud picker
plum bird
lum budder

Certhia familiaris

bark runner
creepy clipper
crawler
speiler
daddy-ike
eeckle
creepet
cuddy
tree mouse

Strix aluco

jinny yewler
jenny hoolet
ivy ullat
hollering
hill hooter
old woman of
the night

Columba palumbus

Too-zoo
cusha
cushie doo
dow doo
timmer doo
queest quest quist
quease
quisty
culver
clatter dove

Pyrrhocorax pyrrhocorax

daw chauk daw
cornish kae
tsauha
tsauha
killigrew
palores

Parus ater

coaly hood
coal hooden
coaly hood
coal hooden
coaly hood
coal hooden
ox-eye

Cuculus canorus

gawky
geck
hobby
gowk
gog gok

Sitta europæa

nut hack
jobber cracker
woodhacker
jobbin
stopper
mud dabber
jar
topper
blue
leg

Caprimulgus europæus

eve churr
razor grinder
heath-jar
dor-moth-gnat hawk
goat sucker
puck bird
goat chaffer
puckeridge
lich fowl
fern owl
gabble ratchet
flying toad

Fulica atra

bald pate
bell poot
white-faced
whistling duck
queet
cute

Parus major

black cap
capped lolly
sit-ye-down
sharp saw
ox-eye
heckymal
tom noup

Carduelis carduelis

sprink
goud sprink
gooldspink
gool French
sheriff's man
foolscoat
thistle warp
moleneck
redcap
seven coloured
flame of the wood
draw water
lady with the twelve flounces

Apus apus

jack squealer
screek
swing devil
skeer devil
devil shrieker
devil squeaker
devil swallow
devil's bitch
cran
whip
devilton

Troglodytes troglodytes

cutty stumpit
wranny wrannock
scutty skiddy
cuddy
tintie
titmeg
cracket
chitty jitty
juggy
puggie
gilliver
stag
our lady's hen

Picus viridis

sprite
spack
wood hack
pie knacker
woodwale
hew hole
pick-a-tree
nicker pecker
high hoe
yaffler
yappingale
hecco eccle
kazek
popinjay
green-peak
wet-wet
yuckel

Gallinula chloropus

morant
stankie
cuddy
kitty
bilcock
bilter
dabchick
nightbird
skitty

Turdus viscivorus

muzzel
mizzly dick
skirlock
skrike
gawthrush
corney
keevor
big felt
jeremy joy
crakle
felfit
bunting
marble
butcher bird

Coturnix coturnix

wet-my-feet
weet-my-feet
wet-my-lip
quick-me-dick
wet weather
but-for-but
throsher
quailzie
deadchick

Sturnus vulgaris

sheppie shepster
sheeprack
sheep stare
black steer
shepstare
starnel
black felt
jacob

Parus cœruleus

predn-play
pridden pral
pinchem
heckymal
allecampagne
spick
nun
billy bee
yaup

Marian Hangings

A Byrd of America

breast wove w winter-cure mustard
   park bench uv a beak
caw rue rainy-day feathers
   left right up-north nest
webbing inta dreamcatchers

Marigold Turning to the Sun

Maria-metal quite contrary
   strength draws
sun's lips slewed adroop
     not following lower things
comes a cropper
   sky blew yelping
  dog-eyed

Palm Tree and Tortoise

scatter enemies while you may
  be a tree sticking out sore
thumbs and cruciforms prettily
   arranged you sprouts a horny
trunk to gladden hoity-tortoise

Mary–Marie me

'Sa virtu m'atire'
motto immersed in anagram
   omen a name my fountains
play before dark stately
homes in caging octagon
 needled crown thralls
  t'thistl'd ownd

The Hand and Pruning Book

'virtue flourishes by wounding'
   my gift of love cut-c
      lean fruity through

Pheasant

      game
    is a shifty word
      it
    movers between
       sights
  as every bird knows how
    to sucker eggs:
 never trust a moving bush

Delphine

dauphin dolphin
   archin' through a stitched-up
  porthole
 being mammal is a but
smelling the colour of
   something
      fishy:
 never tryst a fixed grin

Phoenix

'in the end is my beginning'

Aside

Dee: As concerning the Vision
which yesternight was presented
(unlooked for)
the appearing of the very sea,
and many ships thereon,
and the cutting of the hed of a woman,
by a tall blak man,
what we are to imagin thereof?

Ur(iel): The one did signifie the provisions
of forrayn powers
against the welfare of this land:
which they shortly put into practice.
The other,
the death of the Queene of Scotts.
It is not long unto it.

John Dee 8th May 1583

Mary Through the Looking Glass

A world without humour cannot be serious.

Droll things happened
on ma way to
grief of spleen:

World shut up shop.
Transactions soiled.
A *CloseD* sign got pinned
to m' forehead.

Ma brain must tweak
new avenues to-toy
a-amuse-ma-jaded
humours.

Another day ssLops—
backsides of animals
m-massive with
good riddance—

the midden of the mind
stanks in its tricks

I walk through walls
  I walk through walls
    I walk through walls . . . *Je traverse les murs*
                    Je traverse les murs
                Je traverse les murs
at any time
one plus one
equals
limbo limbo.

Ma *frantic fools*
female jesters and
innocents
long gone—

ma lips chap and mouth with
unlicked dribs of
moonings and swannings and
nerve-edged-nibbles
                         the little gets so 'ittle I hope
                                                          far . . .

Walls hurt my face
they're a too brittle trick
for the unghosted flesh.

I sit and unpick
veins to get at you and
undo my body—

I'm sick of sick
(my mouth mouths)
I'm sick of sick . . . j'en ai marre du mal
                         j'en ai marre du mal

I'm

Mary Through The Looking Glass . . .

Mmms-wrens sin sweetie.
Bugaboo my lugs hear it.
Map my eyes in you.
Arrest.
Toe-holds. Carpe diem.
Grrr-masques.
The longed-n the hurt-n the fell'd.
Bless
O
Bess
ma curfew out this mirror flew through.

Wiregrass cuts a barb.
Greeters far—I mean nooky-aye
it's a tear before bed every neet.

Dumb light squeers dumb dark
j'accuse
you face
you face
you many two utter-matterings
huff breath
scar-f-words
j'accuse
hob-torrent
totem-face
totem-face
            >beak>fronted>
cheeks-a-slope
moove m-o-o-v-e

terse up-river through yr
veer o soot-sheen
gat a cool clear
gat a cool.

Inched near larking norm.
Tokens of love-past
                    fly-past
blue bonnet feathers
f'r his
blue fools ~~~

—rabbit skin
rabbit skin
to wrap ma baby David in—

skeins of white
shot with
intermittent
bombazine

lush hunts

infinite deer
five wolves
some roes
many men
no fish—

quondam queen
quandary queen

many men
no fish.

Ma panting mirror-breath
bars ma
entry.
Ma worried mist clags rank.

Could kill a boar
a man but
couldn't kill a fish
the gasping
mouth of mirror
is endless
gawp of sprat.

() (o) () (o) () (o) () (o)

Bed heirs
ya sad fries
of carnal feast—
ya looms of misery
to un-wombed
posterity.

Do we not lobotomise worrisome fruit?
Furious life fest
countercultured
life forced to kill.

This IS **no** AGE to **be** IN **sane** IN.

Madness is all the rage.

Nobility drop like blossoms
into soft-brained
heaven.

Ma Prison of Extreme Oblivion
is
n-*now*
with fretting and fooming
and unprintable harangues.

Destination dressed with
natal plosions.

Where be the belly-button to press me owt.

Ferryman
ya nabob
let me snorer till noon
a-sleep out ma alien
share
o time weft.

Ma mirror brought prophecies
all night long

forensic cleansing

not one spot
    one iota
of my
blood-to-be
preserved.

Scrub out relics
and a thousand grow
splintered into
ultra precious.

(everyone dreads a
modern-day martyr on
the other side)

Beware le wrung hands
clasped
and sweating
beneath
glory ahhhhhh
ayemen.

My I

I enter you fringe-dressed.

Mirror-mirror.

Oui!

How they worried back home.

Furore biddy nannykins
in omnefarious 'larmings:
Mon Dieu
those animal skins—
if you call that a-dressing
mi missy I'll ouster
thee now—

n-*now* is non-stop nithering wind

raw nipples.

Wearing gay-gear in the face of
Knave Death.

Ha-haa! I see behind mi blindfold—

meniscus amours
somnolent
meniscus amours
somnolent

T'sew is t'breathe.
T'look is t'see between
fingers—
I saw nothing upon nothing.
(J'ai vu rien sur rien.)
Ma mirror crows cruel with
stare-back.

Tonight I cannot pass
my bloodshot eyes.

I cannot pass
my eyes on
to anyone.

I must see what I see.
(Je dois voir ce que je vois)

IamIam**I**am**I**amafraid.

Bibliomancer learns undoer news.
The dread of fallsteps dreads
the fall.

Upon all heads so be it.

Beware m-e-mirror
look out.

Fast-forward centuries on . . .

minnows
quicksilver downing
poisonous poisson
with two-faced gait
they blame on
women's weeee
what's new pussycat
whooooooa whooooaaa.

Nil-be-mouth-breath.

Ma mirror shrinks.
Won't allow my
nightly drown in cockatrice and
parakeets.

Balk!
Am almost
bawd as a billiard ball
so le swim'll win well
in a Buxton
orgasmic
spa.

Mary woz ere!
I scratched in glass.

Ah mariner of mi mirror
it's as much as water can do—
to be
creaseless as hot tea
soothe out ma sores.

Oh how me could murder
alopecia.

I kiss my lips
and pass through you.

Werms fer b-lunches.

Whad am I talkin?

Quail eggs. I bathe in vats of quail eggs.
And wine.
My voice cracks with dry yolk.

Yellow leather.

Shouldn't have
run him through
with my hooking horn
so big
and tidal landing me
here with *her*
that must be *obeyed*
which *isn't me*—
a hopalong haunt of
queeny ways clop
clip-perty clip-perty
clip-perty clip-perty

B ah spoof!
taffeta taffeta
ma mirror rots with
suet and meat trims.

A bilge of offal but why
when
blud is quicker
on the inside
do you not send bouquets?

What is this what?
Which witch dreamt it?
Fabulous monsters ma bottom
a-feely
my eye runs red and linear.

I crave knees-up in France:
I crave a rigadoon.

G-frosh—n–ice.

Not much hot meaty.
Modesty and metal
slip out of hand.

A pool of stealth forms
at my feet.

Melt me frosted mirror.

Let me in!
(Fais-moi entrer!)
So foul a shipwreck
is my heart
the birds within
my ribcage
flutter up-upon
skipt beats.

Exposed to all the winds
and injuries of heaven
only
sly can butt
remorse
that uppers
rampant.

Goosier ma steps through
looking you.
Mi-rrow mi-rrow.
The queen of plum cakes
ruckles my corsets
—a weaponry beyond Exocets—
now there's a word I've never
heard except through you.

I score a time-flashed territory.

Bring up a choir of ages.
My pelvic bones span Minsters—
misericord men nibble mean
leaves.

The craziest paved path
engraved in brave waffle.

Diversions of exorbitant unicorns.

Hoofing hungs of chessmen.

Fleur de lis and fauna fabula.

Woos and ogles.

Go earth just so—aaw—

here comes gruel to snap me out.

Delicacies girdle faux pas.

Crocked unwashed pinkie.

Ginger-*ginger*
queen of subtraction
take loaf by knife—
take pottage by spurtle
cut crust

spoon my neck

escape is caked-up to canker.

Distemper lopped sooner than sadder
will do.

Appearances bleed to edginess.

I detest polled horns and branch.

Bring gracious gowns.
(Apportez des robes gracieuses)

A string of dropped-pearls.
(Un fil de perles pleurées)

I will not a tuckle look—

even through the glass.

～

en ma fin gît mon commencement

Que suis-je hélas? Et de quoi sert ma vie?
Je ne suis fors qu'un corps privé de cœur,
Une ombre vaine, un objet de malheur
Qui n'a plus rien que de mourir en vie.
Plus ne me portez, O ennemis, d'envie
A qui n'a plus l'esprit à la grandeur.
J'ai consommé d'excessive douleur
Votre ire en bref de voir assouvie.
Et vous, amis, qui m'avez tenue chère,
Souvenez-vous que sans cœur et sans santé
Je ne saurais aucune bonne œuvre faire,
Souhaitez donc fin de calamité
Et que, ici-bas étant assez punie,
J'ai ma part en la joie infinie.

Mary Stuart

The Scottish Queen's Cypher Alphabet

bye

gy

Womes

Meath

Hasy

Oree

foads

aeart

Ot

Oaunts

Anow

Rove

Oy

Oot

Xpaque

OOetticoat

:uick

Ribbon

Vtir

terror

⊥nder

⊥iew

Ⅱith

Ⅶenophobic

Oah

roo

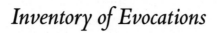

Inventory of Evocations

Stomacher

squashed and drawn
quarters
plunging
ribs
into
lungs into heart
into
minced-sweet-meats
gives a fit of
spleen
unseen
distortions
from a fattening queen's
belly ache
something
had to give
the
upsurging
arches
a
space
for
a
gothic
revival
of
eyebrows

Silk Stockings

luxury
earth dogs
ruck
ankles
deepcut
v
varicose
terriers
truss't up
thighs
lie
in
disregarded
post-inelegant
demolition
of the
egg
box

Satin Slippers

petite
crusht-ice
slippers-petal
a
foot
ah
an
other foot
too drunk
to ease
the
ornamental
weight
of
ages
shod
and
trod
oh
our life
is rock
and
odd
to
the stocks
and
jammed-up
toes

Slashed Sleeves

my pen
staggereth
my hand
at an up
the
sliver
o
silver
baulks
the
buckram
raw
elbow
forms
a de
formed
'Y'

What's in the Cabinet of the Said Lady?

Two snake-tongues
Water-cinnamon
cinder-water
t' wither
phantom limbs dumb-
drowning dram
  One hanging-horn
brimmed neat
powdered unicorn
spindle dasht to shards
  Spikenard
Barley of mowed-meadows
stewed and sieved
for clear spring-time
urine
  Four golden fruit bowls
Bad-blood dried
stock-still in more blood
stone dreg-mired
green shot magic
  A lady chasing cupid
Stone-toad
lode-hoard
done-away doom
unloaded
  An emblem pressed through a comb
Toad-stone
domed asteroid
looming side pain
unwound in sidereal
  A crystal mirror with fire flares
A silver key to unwind
stars or
banish some soul
with a body attached

A mother o pearl lion
Pearl in a ring ~ noctilucent
as a post-war
Del Monte
tinned pear ~ noctilucent
    A lance in a roll with fire-flames
Tigers-eyes with properties
beyond the see
stave-off psychic
weather storms
    A wee enamelled dog
Gold phial clasping a stone
soriety-fuel feud
pips resin in
marrow
    Two favour ribbons—torched and lanced
Filigree metal
intermeddled
hangers for burnt-out
stretched ears
    A pigeon and a parakeet
Opal set sits ~ marvels
how divers are
gladdened by an unstable
prescience
    A golden lamb is stool pigeon is informer is white fluffy cloud
Curio and curiouser ~ a cloth
of state
unwound and unwrit
in Sheffield City Centre
    An Indian apple bugged with rubies and turquoise

84

Dressed to Die For

Black satin dress broidered w'blacker velvet
a body

Jet set-faced acorn buttons hewn
a heart torn away

Purple trim of wimberry stain
a vain shadow

White lace-edged veil touching earth
death-in-life

Blue stockings silver-edged
overwhelming grief

Black Spanish leather shoes
asking misery to cease

Green silk garters
punished in a world like this

Crimson petticoat
my portion in eternal bliss

PART THREE

Shed

Without my shed-builders Alan, Bob, David and Jin,
Part Three would be a shedding without a shed.

GM

Outer Apparition

from the kitchen sink
the outer is lacerated w/ blinds.
Yellow . . . /
            z-yellow . . . /
                        z-s-lattered . . . /

What is called *golden*
depresses
to *umber*
under viral dusk
                static
quakes its seeable walls
windows
            warping door
the roof assumes
a brazen slope   neck down
            rump up
    an inverted 'v' sign
            cheeky
marigold gloves lie used and lewd
a yellow duster playing dead on
a ledge near my left elbow
dares to brush it with
overfamiliar
                creep
creepy
        creepers
    tentacle colours

gang.

Inner Sanctum

What seeps in 'n' out of knot-holes?

............w..h..i..s..p..s..........
.............w..a..s..p..s............

Inaudible messages from outer
trumpetings vibrate
      cranny insects
money-spiders
     dosh…..dosh
ratcheting nut carpings
    detached eyeballs
          o' spoowks
louche fingers
         stiffening
draughts
positions of light imitating
         blonde eyelashes
   an unblink
murder of
    imagined bird
      beak
 o

  o

   of Luna beam at double noon
shoot out
     the unseasoned bleed of
  resin
a variety of stigmatas
      invisible
pollutants too dangerous
to list
    the name of the day
       better not dwelt on.

Block 'em up.

Close the Perspex windows.

Infestation

500 tonnes equals
bio-hazard sludge-upping
North Sea gizzard
casting
wholesides
of our Isles
darker
than
shark-shadow
stealth
contaminating
night-scented
stocks
listinglisting
arthritic
ghost ships
denser that
woder
      water
         watter
non-solvable
mercy-all
leadleadleadleadleadlead
mercury
chromium
cadmium
asbestos
spumed peeling
painted throat.

Heading for Mandyland.

Shut that door!

Amble

Perspex is not the
incomparable sashay of bombé glass

Do not stay still in front of her curves

the diamond slasht
                        light
trussed at angles
            coming at you
at all ways
            side-jaw'd
in a shudder of
                absinthe
a twist of
                eau-de-nil
and f-fake prophecy

Do not stay still in front of her curves

promenade the
long room of
Haddon Hall—
do it with hands on hips ~
gavotte it! ~!~~!~

time

travels

the 21st century is ill
at ease
the Euphrates
in conflict
running out of sorts
thins to
thinner than

lavender water
and f-fake prophecy.

Dead electric.

A surge through
the marrow bone
picks up the migration of
animal spirits.

Metempsychosis ✕ 3

With profound incident
fabric absorbs
spilt emotion
contracting pulse into
traumatised
relic
a drop of blood
                    whispering
behind a screen
                    flickering
'Is there any metaphoric body there?'

×✕×

The migration of soul
holds a breath between
tooth and
beak
if
I
could mouth a sound
to form an
I
it would say
my claw
my claw
has been
hurting for days—
if I could count the *days*—
I would call out for *drugs*.

×✕×

Between the body and the text
a gulf tript with
razor wired ghosts—
trickt-up luminous forms.

Germination

The mind as oubliette can
shut out all mewling
howling
terror haunts and guilt.

Cycling towards
the next century starts
the second the next century starts
with nowhere near a cure for
the common cold credit card
harassing
junk
conflicts.

I need to find a seed tray:

sow 'n' grow a perfect wall.

If we rid the world
of territorial
desire would it
would it
bang to rights—
would I
would I
share my shed?

Out of Africa:

'It was war we weren't blowing kisses'

Not much shack shelter
in those words
for the limping
armless
         lipless
and gang-got.

Crypt
O
words
with the first solving of the day
the sun re-cities the earth
and blots the necropolis.

Wooden walls
flim-timbre
      tinder
         cinder.

Perspex windows
self-scratch
in the night.

The door lock is not
pickproof.

The alarm bells unbought.

This is no place to hide
from civil conflict

high minded winds

f-fake realities.

Cultivation

Shedding-out all alone
on mi-own me-me-be-binge
scarpering
a paper crusade for
the decline of Siberian tigers:
their statistics poke through
stronger than
their fading halitosis.

Things to stress out precious leisure hours.

Birds crucifly—
blown off course
ina wild
updraught of
heat loss
from
balding
conglomerate brains.

Overlook
the fractured
hanging of
butterfly wings
on a grand scale
monitor lizards
take cold-blooded
notes
      (with a sound like
       red cherries
       to swoon to
       it is hard to go global
       on a bright winter's morning)

estranged words
fly from
overheated faces
migrating to
continents
on the other side of
smoked glass
stretched-out-limos.

Interlude

My love loves pickled walnuts.
My love loves pickled walnuts in port.
My love loves pickled walnuts in port with brandy.

Prune

Voicewarps
in butterwraps of
sound
    bites
     into
burgeoning
        spine-ache
the need for tongue-tzip
lime cordial
and black sun
flower
     seeds for my
uncaged birds tzsu-tzsu
a soft-soul shuffle
into sidereal leery night
I pick up the
name Shakespeare
and gather
another
crop
of avoidable
tragedies
drove-by
shooting
black night
beauties.

Interlude

My love loves lamb's liver.
My love loves lamb's liver in wine.
My love loves lamb's liver in wine with wine.

Pa(x)

Many centralisations
                    across the universe:
Andromeda in a spin.
Nether Edge slippin
dow
n its
o
  w
    n
*hi*l
    l
sk
i
n.
The virgin statue leaking
                    weeps in
                        Venezuela.
The corner shop.
A dark bar.
Some field.
Every bus stop.
Texas over
a barrel.
Burma in the
doldrums.
            Ang Sang Sui as ever under house arrest:
Flowers
        hang fire
                in her tied-out hair.

inherhair

Bloodsuch
            eye of Mars
ahems
        on Earth—

after weeks of clear skies
clouds
       perverse
beneath
blocked horizons of contempt—
as if *we* care—
eye-poking
teeth-extroothing
amputation
is an ongoing
gong-gifter
a swash of derring-do
so be gone
mythical mads &
planetary charismatics
    — yo —
   — love —
don't live here
   anymore

Sidereal time emphasizes
reversed profiles:
(or so it says on the back of
my imaginary pack of cards)
pink lint and gauze
re-verse in-verse
draw a load of
pesterers along the rind
of raw.

Is it too late
or too early
in worldstory
to talk seriously
about
ticky emotions?

Dark strutters lept icebreakers.
Happy-sads skim purring hurt.
A lept-frogging all intellect
leaves
outstanding orders to wilt out
the bleeding heart.

Amend August :
bicker-out invasion planning
drift-ift to September
without maim

It's a start.

O

It's an

A

Blessing the Throat

Blaise beheaded saint
  deliver hush poorly swallows
    goitre-gnomes
        whooping cough up inner-ginnels
          wool combers thrum-ashreds
            hackled animals wild
          teaselled seadogs
      bier beasts
ululating stonecutters
tooth-aching mason marks
  bitter passion
    bawming the thorn
      bone of fish
        stuck down little lad's
          singing lane
            the day before candle mass
            St Andrew's cross
            flames two-pronged a-tine
          each side of gurning throat
        the buttercup shines your love of utter
      yeller sounds a cur a bleed of wave we carry on
we've started so we'll fan out hope that embers
  go to pieces elsewhere in the blaze of
Blaise belov'd beheaded saint

Echo Visions

A mischief
            (chief (sheaf
breeding up
            (up (pup (p
a monster
            (amongst (angst (tear
proud
        (owd (dowd (dud
unreasonable
                (treasonable (able
laughter
        (after (raft
the precipice
                (ice (eyes (sus
drags
        (rags
slaves
        (aves
walking
        (awk (aw (king
on the wild
            (while (ill (d

side

house of terrestrial
angels rage out of this
world

when phantoms drone
down the air waves
too strained an attention
might hurt the head

Azeal the angel is overworked
addressing the apostrophe

The
                eye
                        not
                                named
                                        cannot sleep

point of lure
glass of lyre
steep of grace
skying fly night un
                soul-steeple flow
glass of lure
point of lyre
steep of grace

The
                ear
                        not
                                called
                                        cannot burn

if they move
on a half-lit city street—
what can scare us more than a
pair of dropped white gloves?

Interlude

My love loves dates.
My love loves dates with figs.
My love loves dates with significant figs.

Fear of Prophecy & Failed Stars

Haute couture
is not a doctrine—
but nothing is more rigorous
than
n..^^^//.../^^...!eed!ework
teachers
tugging
at
your
bust darts >>>>>>>>>>
making you
        un*pick **k k k***

Was this ordained:
An unstitching of life?
A learning curvature
hardening shy buds?

The answer is upside
down on the back page
of an unwritten book.

Without a doubt
the hanging baskets hang
until dislodged.

Unrest of rinds
peely outers rucking to runes.
Brain minding the games
minding the you.

Lightyears yeasting.

starlightstarlight

simple barriers arise
//////////////////
the imposition of constellations
scaling
heart-broke windows

skylightskylight

the radio backdrop
misbakes
Syria with Serious with Sirius

(there is low
talk of a failed star)

across the city a kitchen prophet levitates
above babble lamenting
the closure of tea bags:
if loose leaf Yorkshire Tea is
from Assam, Africa and Ceylon
do the leaves talk Tyke?

And then the thought occurs:
what bird is a But-for-But?

Is that a But-for-But on that
all-for-all-that tree?

Rusk rottings lies on lips
hoar rims the mug
risk of risk of risk of . . .
Prime Minister's question time
—the goonshow in
              the growmore dark—
the blood and bone and fishy
smells turn my shed
into abbatoir.

Time to feed the roses.

Scattered stitched-up loops.

Interlude

My love loves soft-boiled eggs.
My love loves soft-boiled eggs in china.
My love loves soft-boiled eggs in china in Sheffield.

Badly Faked Flowers

starlightstarlight

words in the out-there world
beyond the gables
and non-existent gate
strung-out high on pitch
'gonna gonna gonna . . . blah . . . you'
Oh go on then—
show me
'cerebral'
tattooed on your
nether parts.

I block you out with
kitsch from Bruges
Pendle and Madrid—
Manx feathers
everybeach pebbles
Makonde from Africa
and a
trembling green table
on terms with all the tumuli
across my planetary face.

But where are the
badly faked flowers
buried
years ago for
loitering
too long in their plastic
dead heat of plagiarism?
Is the answer in this
quote
around another corner
of hearing:

'some come year after year to embroider stone'

Interlude

My love loves gargoyles.
My love loves gargoyles in rain.
My love loves gargoyles on the Seine in rain.

The Comforting

A greater shroud of comfort none:
to screw one's little head in
fad brocading curtains and
spin atwist twill it grips
t'head to a pulse a-tock
and *ou* blood a bove
to pin point comfort
cornet van-it-as
green sleeve is
melba deca
dant e
cutty
ice
po
o
le
its
atop
feely
thinga
with roots
skinny fibres
forensic thin a live
stain the *what* inside linen
in a thread of so lovely writ
flimsy as nerve tissue cumulus
when angels cross the noon chant
Angelus gushty ups the gymslip shiver.

The Flouncing

left hand crow in her howl tree
in my not-my garden one grows
sadder faces by night
aggregate surfacing
beauty and value
it gotto be
mucked-up brassy-mink
stalls low turtle
doves coo-**do** on fowls a-pleasure feeding
little cheeps **of**-*a* **of**-*a* **of**-*a*
prisonprism
wearing
flounced osseous wishbine
eat time mi dear
till it fills a stocking to tangerine
dates mi darling
quail eggs and kumquats
stuff white bread faces
bleached unto death **coo**-do
I dream again Manchurian
sikka deer smelling
apricots the Abbess of Unreason
levels the Lady of Misrule
conjoined symbiosis paranorm-floats
modulation **of**-*a* **of**-*a* **of**-*a* **a**-*of* each thought folly
goes north a block to my jugular larkspurs
in full frontal glottis inflame
the late summer lucifers
flock my swallow with
globus-hystericus

Queen of the Bean

Ms Rule's over baked kake
        ////
cloved aleatory
upside middle
mess down
blewd letting
anarchy
run
a
mock stag
amid the stations
of the rank pullers
            ////
                tumbling
with neck ruff spangled to
shun out this world
Queen Bean
lifts her skirt
à la rhinestone cowboy
showing ankle spurs
in an animal stamp
            ////
                dance
with attitude

beasts and birds
baked in a pie
four and twenty
pudding-black
virus-free frogs ride
drumsticks on wings
breaking the mould
          ////
            humming
hymns to mortality
       sorrowmyrrhsorrow
       sorrowmyrrhsorrow
myrrh-pie pudding-be
plum and date reap fest
        ////
presentation of the salt on
seasoned wag of tipped-tongue.

(So many blossoms on our tree
and not one apple uptit)

Interlude

My love loves sleeping.
My love loves sleeping with sleep.
My love loves sleeping with sleep with me.

Opus Anglicanum

(movement)

taunts sewn daily
beaming
a cluster
of ad-ages: history history history
will be sore-winged with
selective forgiving

A cast shedding envy
throughout Europe. oui ya sí
we gave them
a needling to die for
couching ore sprigs
into brand ancient chasubles of awe
so much so they named it after us
       O-Opus Anglicanum
'England is for us surely a garden
of delights—an inexhaustible well'—
so sang Papa Innocent to our choral copes
and mitres.

what beauty we unravelled

(movement)

With every fibre of spin
Ministers of Misrule
thread-paint moral empires on their
sleeves. pink pink pink
go the shears at the wrists
on the edge of the wood

secular embroidery
—*what stands still long enough*—
catches trappings
banners palls purses
underneath and hidden linen
outre vestments
couched bed hangings
misleading cushions
runners
lips lying in wait
you name it
              O
          Opus!
and a pair of shin-new
leg-long buskins found
in a power-tomb in Canterbury
where a cathedral is

still

a metre of petersham
will
stiff out a great coat
with
sham to spare for
fair war

just

(movement)

stuckup on thorn hedge
hemmed in
broderie anglaise
capped
pearlies kink the may day
blossom floss
a fly pass is
buzzing her maj
at enormous expense
the sky streaks red white
blue
on blue

Intelligence born in sour light
cramps eyes guiding the gilt ~
a sequence of sequins
is a chain of glitzer
on the slope
going blind for an
          anthem is a song
                              too high
on a hot bright morning in
a strained voice
he sang
across the waters:

'we have not yet found shiny
pointy things we call weapons'

expert
embroiderers
finger their bodkins
weaving empires

upon time

threads get knotted

Dong! The history drowns.

ACKNOWLEDGEMENTS

Individual poems or complete sections of *Escafeld Hangings* first appeared
in the following magazines and anthologies:
Ahadada Reader 1, The Gig # 12, Call:Review, Twenty Six, Chicago Review
and on the following websites:
The Alterran Poetry Assemblage, Electronic Poetry Review, Gut Cult Issue 3/4,
Nth Position, The Drunken Boat, Masthead, How2.

She Kept Birds was first published by Slack Buddha Press.

Mary Through the Looking Glass and *Marian Hangings* were first published by
Gargoyle Editions.

The Scottish Queen's Cypher Alphabet was first exhibited at the Oculus Visual Poetry
Biennial in Japan.

The following have provided invaluable source material. My thanks also to any I
have failed to mention for their glimpses of rare truffles in the undergrowth.
Books and pamphlets:
John Daniel Leader, *Sheffield Castle and Mary Queen of Scots*
Antonia Frazer, *Mary Queen of Scots*
James Mackay, *In My End is My Beginning*
Roy Strong & Julia Trevelyan Owen, *Mary Queen of Scots*
J. Keith Cheetham, *Mary Queen of Scots: The Captive Years*
T. Walter Hall, *Incunabula of Sheffield*
David Clarke, *Strange South Yorkshire*
Francesca Greenoak, *All the Birds of the Air*
B. Ronald Dyson, *A Glossary of Old Sheffield Trade Words and Dialect*
Ian B. Cowan (compiled and edited), *The Enigma of Mary Stuart*
Margaret Swain, *The Needlework of Mary Queen of Scots*
Norah & William Montgomerie (collected and edited), *Scottish Nursery Rhymes*
Elizabeth Eisenberg, *This Costly Countess Bess of Hardwick*
Elizabeth Eisenberg, *The Captive Queen in Derbyshire*

Websites:
Mary Queen of Scots: Official Website
Historical Costumes
Sheffield Markets: A History of Sheffield Castle
Catholic Encyclopaedia
Gode Cookery

I would particularly like to thank my dear friends Ligia Roque for her translations of the French and inspirational singing, Glenn Storhaug for his perfection with a contagious smile and Alan Halsey for his enduring support and boundless knowledge.

Last but by no means least my liberal use of the letters, poems and the exemplary eloquence under adversity of Mary Stuart, Queen of the Scots. Merci.

Credits and acknowledgements for the *Mary Through the Looking Glass* CD

Performed by Geraldine Monk and Ligia Roque

Que suis-je hélas? Mary Stuart / Ligia Roque

Lágrima Amália Rodrigues / Carlos Gonçalves

Tive um Coração, Perdi-o Amália Rodrigues / Fontes Rocha

Recorded in 2005 by Charlie Collins at the Sound Kitchen, Sheffield